The Healthy Hedonist

NICOLE HERFT

is a food stylist, author and private chef who
has worked in the UK and Australia.
She has always been passionate about superfoods,
smoothies and juices and has worked
with many top chefs and food writers.
She currently works on cookbooks,
cookery shows, magazines and films and
is the author of *Little Italy*.

The Healthy Hedonist

40 Naughty but
Nourishing Cocktails
by **Nicole Herft**

Photography by Nassima Rothacker

Kyle Books

TO MY MUM, FOR IMPARTING HER NUTRITIONAL WISDOM ON ME!

First published in Great Britain in 2016
by Kyle Books, an imprint of Kyle Cathie Ltd
192-198 Vauxhall Bridge Road
London SW1V 1DX
general.enquiries@kylebooks.com
www.kylebooks.com

10 9 8 7 6 5 4 3 2 1

ISBN 978 0 85783 390 7

Designer: Giulia Garbin
Photographer: Nassima Rothacker
Cover illustration: Ohn Mar Win
Food Stylist: Nicole Herft
Props Stylist: Lydia Brun
Project Editor: Sophie Allen
Editorial Assistant: Hannah Coughlin
Production: Nic Jones, Gemma John and Lisa Pinnell

A Cataloguing in Publication record for this title
is available from the British Library.

Colour reproduction by ALTA, London
Printed and Bound in China by 1010 International Printing Ltd.

HAVE FUN, BUT PLEASE DRINK RESPONSIBLY

CONTENTS

INTRODUCTION

The Healthy Hedonist – well… that's pretty much me!

Healthy sometimes and definitely the hedonist at times too. This book is designed to show you that you can enjoy your naughty cocktails in a 'healthier' way.

I'm here to show you that you really don't need to use lots of sugary syrups and liquors and fizzy, sugar-filled mixers to make a drink taste amazing. I've cut out any added refined sugar from these recipes because I can. There are alternatives that can be even more delicious and nutritious at the same time – trust me!

My mum introduced me to juicing at around the age of 7. She was, and still is to this day, one of the healthiest people I know. We weren't allowed sweets, crisps, cordial, chocolate or fizzy drinks at all in our house. At the time, I probably didn't really appreciate what she was doing, but as an adult she has paved a great path for me. I've always been a chef and over-indulging is just a part of my job as well as my nature, but because Mum taught me about nutrition and its benefits at such a young age I feel I have the knowledge to create some balance – well I try to anyway!

I worked as a chef in Australia from the age of 17. I started in Italian restaurants, but was also interested in whole foods and cooked at quite a few vegetarian places before settling in at Decadence, a predominantly vegetarian health food café and juice bar. Everyday, I would create different juice combinations. I found that creating these flavour combinations for juices worked in exactly the same way as food, but I would also think about the nutrients and try to make them both vegetable and fruit based.

I moved to London at the age of 23. I thought I would find a cool vegetarian café and juice bar to work in, but back in 2001 they just didn't exist! So I ended up working as a chef and part-time as a bartender. I worked at 'Harlem' in Notting hill – it was owned by the American music producer, Arthur Baker. It was here that I learnt all about the classic cocktails, which really interested me. I also worked at Favela Chic in Shoreditch with the coolest and craziest bunch of Brazilians that I have ever met. We had the best time and served a really fruity and sugary array of cocktails there. They were delicious but oh… the sugary hangovers – ouch!

So, basically, the idea for this book comes from my experience making cocktails, but also from my love of juicing. These cocktails combine the two in the best possible way. I've only used natural sweeteners like agave nectar, maple syrup, coconut palm sugar and honey in these babies. You'll be surprised at how much sweetness real fruit contains.

I encourage you to try to cut down your intake of refined sugars. When sugar is processed, it's depleted of all the nutrients and minerals, so what you are left with is a refined carbohydrate or 'empty calories'. The problem is our bodies can't utilise or digest this substance. This is why we get a sugar shock – it's the sugar leaching all the nutrients and minerals within our body, in its demand for digestion. Without going into too much detail, you need to understand that it's toxic for our bodies. There are so many other choices these days that make it easier to cut down than ever before.

Now I can't control the fact that booze will contain certain amounts of sugar, but I've tried where possible to use alcohol that's lower in sugars. There are a few liquors in the book, but I also show you how to make your own fruit-based syrups.

Unfortunately, in our society, sugar = happiness! It's always a part of celebrations, birthdays and rewards. It's a hard habit to break, but we can do it. I've never seen people be more conscious about health food, drinks and lifestyle as they are right now. It's hard to separate what is good and what isn't, but at the end of the day, if you are eating things that are fresh, organic and natural and you are preparing them from scratch, yourself I think you are doing alright. My ethos is that it's all about balance at the end of the day.

Now if you are entertaining, and let's face it, if you make delicious cocktails, you're always playing the host, all of these recipes can be multiplied to serve more people. The popsicles are great for entertaining, as you can make a few batches of them in advance. Let them freeze, remove them from their moulds, wrap them in clingfilm and keep in the freezer.

GETTING DOWN TO THE NITTY GRITTY!

As a chef, I truly believe you can only make delicious food or drinks with great ingredients.

When buyng your fruit and vegetables – try to choose organic if you can. What's the point of trying to be healthier if your ingredients have been sprayed with loads of chemicals and pesticides? This goes for all the other ingredients in this book as well – the nutritional supplements, dried goods, teabags etc. In most cases they will be prepared with more care, taste more delicious and be better for you.

Another really good tip is to start freezing all your ripe fruit when it's in season. Buy fruit when it's on special, which is usually when it is most ripe and pop it in the freezer. I have so much fruit in my freezer: berries, melon, grapes, pineapple chunks, kiwi fruit, bananas. Fruit isn't always at its best when you purchase it so keep it near some bananas, let it ripen and then bag it up and freeze it. I have so many choices then, with what I can do for morning juices and, of course, cheeky cocktails when a few friends drop by.

Now let's talk Equipment.

JUICERS

There are three types of juicers you can buy:

CENTRIFUGAL This is the most common type of juicer and the least expensive. The ingredient is thrown against a high-speed blade – the juice is strained in one end and the pulp in the other to discard. The pulp does contain the majority of the fibre from the ingredient. Now these are the juicers that most people have. They are fast, inexpensive and easy to clean. If you are going for one of these, make sure the shoot is wide (ie. the type that can fit a whole apple) as this will mean less prep time for you. This is the type of juicer I have. I want my juicing time to be quick and easy. If it takes too long to wash or to juice it can feel like a chore and we don't want that. I may lose the fibre, but I still enjoy lots of other nutrients everyday.

MASTICATING This is the type that can extract the juice from wheatgrass. There is a coil inside that grinds the ingredient in order to extract the juice. It's much slower than the centrifugal type and doesn't always leave you with a smooth juice. It's also more difficult to clean but the good news is that it can juice leafy greens and the juice will be richer in nutrients because the pulp isn't separated.

HYDRAULIC / COLD PRESSED This is the top of the range style juicer that you will find in some juice bars and cafés. This machine juices in two stages – the first grinds the ingredient into a pulp and the second extracts all the juice from this pulp. This is the best method for extracting both the most juice and the most nutrients. But let's be honest – it's crazy expensive, large and heavy. It takes a long time to prep, juice and clean, so unless you are opening a juice bar, this is probably not for you!

BLENDERS

There are many types of blenders out there, but I encourage you to try and use a high-powered blender like a Thermomix, Vitamix or Blendtec. They have a motor that runs at over 500 watts. These guys can handle just about anything you throw inside them. They can also deal with large amounts as they have a 2-litre jug capacity. They are all on the expensive side, but I use mine everyday so I feel like I can justify the cost. You can always buy the refurbished/reconditioned ones too which are usually half the price!

The high-speed friction, when using a Thermomix, can actually heat up the contents if left on for a long time. For example, kale is one tough leafy green so if you are blending it for more than 1 minute, always do it with ice cubes or frozen fruit so that it keeps the drink cold. These three machines are the only ones that I have used that can pulverise anything and give you a silky smooth juice in the end. My advice is to research the blender before buying it and look at its reviews. Make sure it can handle ice and that it has a strong motor. Then go for what you can afford.

The information below refers to the ingredients used in my cocktails – not necessarily juicing in general.

FRUIT THAT SHOULD BE JUICED BY HAND

Oranges, Lemons, Limes, Grapefruit – these can be put through a centrifugal juicer as well, but they will have a layer of froth which we don't really want.

FRUIT AND VEG THAT SHOULD BE PUT THROUGH A CENTRIFUGAL JUICER

Cucumber, Carrots, Celery, Apples, Pears, Beetroot, Turmeric root, Ginger, Cabbage, Lettuce, Fennel, Watermelon.

FRUIT AND VEG THAT SHOULD BE BLENDED

Berries, Soft fruit, Apricots, Peaches, Pineapple, Melon, Kiwi fruit, Grapes, Frozen fruit, Bananas, Kale, Spinach, Mint, Herbs, Papaya, Peas, Tomatoes, Cherries, Avocado and Mango.

COCKTAILS SHAKERS

I've used a few different cocktails shakers in my time and they do produce different results. The Boston Shakers are great, especially the ones that come with a glass with measurements on it. I'm also a fan of the metal cocktail shakers. Make sure you get one that is tight fitting and has a strainer incorporated in the pourer.

COCKTAIL STRAINERS

These make life much easier so invest in one if you don't already have one! The Hawthorne strainer is the type that has either two or four prongs sticking out and a semi-circle of springs underneath. It's designed to fit snuggly into a shaker tin, spring-side down. This will hold in all the ice and any solids but will allow froth to come though. It will basically be your new best friend! For an even smoother drink, strain your drink through a small fine mesh strainer – very similar to a tea strainer.

Most importantly, enjoy the love of making cocktails! And experiment, that's the best bit. Use the recipes in this book as inspiration and add your favourite fruit and vegetables and create your own. Mix up the base alcohol and get your friends around to enjoy a better way of drinking. I'd love to see your creations too, so do get in touch with me @eat_love_travel on Instagram and Twitter.

Big love, Nicole x

ICE ICE BABY

So the idea behind this is to simply get more **colour**, more **flavour** and more **nutrients** into your drinks!

You can freeze almost anything into ice-cube trays. Experiment with herbs, edible flowers, fruit and berries. You can also pour coconut water or fruit and vegetable juices straight into the trays or mix them with other ingredients too. It's totally up to you…

Go nuts with shapes and sizes too. I love the heart shapes, star shapes and rod-shaped trays. You can find loads online so get involved!

FRUITYLICIOUS

Cherry Ripe
Peach and Chia Bellini
Iced Mixed Berry Sangria
Raspberry Pisco Smash
Strawberry Caipivodka
Blueberry and Acai Smash
Strawberry and Jasmine Iced Tea
Kombucha Pimms Punch
Pomegranate and Vanilla Cosmo
Thyme Bramble
Pink Champagne and Goji Popsicles

CHERRY RIPE

This silky-smooth drink is inspired by one of my favourite Aussie chocolate treats – the 'Cherry Ripe'. The combination of cherries, chocolate and coconut is highly addictive as I'm sure you'll agree. Apart from being delicious, cherries contain loads of powerful antioxidants. And cacao is said to improve your mood, prevent ageing and give you energy!

SERVES 2
50ml vodka · 40ml cherry brandy
40ml crème de cacao · 80g frozen pitted cherries
50ml tart cherry juice · 30ml maple syrup
2 teaspoons raw cacao powder
100ml coconut cream · Ice cubes
Fresh cherries, cacao nibs and cherry chocolate,
to garnish

EQUIPMENT
High-speed blender and 2 short glasses

Place the vodka, cherry brandy, crème de cacao, frozen cherries and cherry juice into a high-speed blender. Blend for 1 minute – or until completely smooth. Add the maple syrup, raw cacao powder and coconut cream to the blender and blend for a further 30 seconds.

Fill the serving glasses with ice and divide the drink between the glasses. Garnish with a few fresh cherries, a sprinkling of cacao nibs and a strip of cherry chocolate.

PEACH AND CHIA BELLINI

I love a Bellini made with fresh peaches. This version contains tiny little chia seeds, which pack a powerful nutritional punch. They contain loads of antioxidants, fibre, protein and omega-3s. Peaches provide a natural sweetness along with more antioxidants and vitamins.

SERVES 2
80g ripe yellow peach, skin removed
15ml agave nectar • 20ml Aperol
2 teaspoons white chia seeds • 250ml prosecco
Thin wedges of ripe yellow peaches, to garnish

EQUIPMENT
Mini food processor or blender,
2 vintage coupe glasses

Place the peach into a mini food processor or blender along with the agave nectar and Aperol. Blend until smooth. Transfer the purée to a small bowl and stir in the chia seeds. Leave the chia seeds to swell for about 5 minutes.

Divide the peach mixture between the glasses. Half-fill each glass with prosecco and mix well to distribute the peach purée with the prosecco. Top with the remaining prosecco and garnish with a peach wedge.

ICED MIXED BERRY SANGRIA

Sangria is such a lovely summer drink. This refreshing version is packed with fresh raspberries, blueberries, strawberries and blackberries. Berries are full of antioxidants, low in calories, high in nutrients and super delicious!

SERVES 4

300g fresh mixed berries, plus 150g extra for the jug
3 tablespoons agave nectar • Ice cubes or Berry Ice
Cubes (see page 12) • 750ml Rosé Rioja

EQUIPMENT

Small saucepan, Sieve, Cocktail stirrer,
Serving jug and 4 glasses

Place the mixed berries, 200ml water and agave nectar into a small saucepan and bring to the boil. Reduce the heat and allow to simmer for 10-15 minutes. Remove from the heat and pass the mixture though a sieve. Press the berries with the back of a spoon to make sure you get all their juices. Leave the mixture to cool.

Half-fill your jug with ice cubes. Slice the extra strawberries and halve the blackberries and add these, and the other mixed berries, to the jug with the berry syrup and then finally the Rosé Rioja. Stir well and serve.

RASPBERRY PISCO SMASH

This is my spin on a Pisco Sour, which is one of my favourite drinks. This drink is packed with fresh raspberries that are high in phytonutrients and antioxidants.

SERVES 2
80g fresh raspberries · 25ml agave nectar · 80ml pisco (I use Soldeica) 40ml lemon juice · 2 small egg whites · Ice cubes · Extra raspberries, to garnish

EQUIPMENT
Metal cocktail shaker, Muddler and 2 short glasses

Make sure you use a metal cocktail shaker for this drink because it gives you a much better froth. Add the raspberries and agave nectar to the cocktail shaker and muddle until the mixture turns into a pulp. Next add the pisco, lemon juice and egg whites. Pop the lid on and shake like crazy! The more you shake, the better the froth.

Add a few ice cubes to each glass and pour the drink through the lid of the cocktail shaker – the holes are big enough to allow the froth to pour through. Garnish each one with a couple of extra raspberries and enjoy.

STRAWBERRY CAIPIVODKA

Brazilians know how to drink, and this little number is inspired from my days in Rio de Janeiro. If it has a base of cachaca, it's a Caipirinha, but if you want vodka, it's a Caipivodka! This is my strawberry version, with honey and chamomile tea.

SERVES 2
1 chamomile teabag
2 tablespoons orange blossom honey 80g strawberries, hulled and sliced 70ml pink grapefruit juice · Seeds from ½ vanilla pod · 80ml vodka · Ice cubes or Strawberry Ice Cubes (see page 12) · Sliced strawberries and fresh chamomile flowers, to garnish

EQUIPMENT
Cocktail shaker, Muddler, Cocktail strainer and 2 short glasses

Pour 220ml boiling water over the teabag, add the honey and leave to steep for 10 minutes. Remove the teabag and let cool.

Place the strawberries and vanilla seeds in the cocktail shaker. Muddle until they are pulpy and all the juices have been released. Add the grapefruit juice and vodka and 2 handfuls of ice cubes. Shake vigorously for 1 minute and strain into glasses that have been filled with strawberry ice cubes. Garnish with strawberries and chamomile flowers.

BLUEBERRY AND ACAI SMASH

Berries contain high amounts of phytochemicals that are naturally occurring nutrients that protect our cells from damage. They are also said to keep you mentally sharp and lower your blood pressure. Acai is said to boost your energy levels and your sex drive and is also great for your heart, skin and immune system. All of this, along with some bubbles – what's not to love?!

SERVES 4
100g fresh blueberries · 30ml agave nectar · 12 fresh mint leaves
2 teaspoon organic acai powder or 50g thawed
acai pulp · Ice cubes or Blueberry and Mint
Ice Cubes (see page 12) · 75ml gin (I like Bombay Sapphire)
75ml Manderine Napoléon · 30ml lemon juice
400ml prosecco · Blueberry skewers and extra
blueberries, to garnish

EQUIPMENT
Cocktail shaker, Muddler, Cocktail stirrer,
Serving jug and 4 glasses

Place the blueberries, agave nectar, mint leaves and acai into a large cocktail shaker and muddle well.

Half-fill the cocktail shaker with ice, then add the gin, Mandarine Napoléon and lemon juice. Shake vigorously for 1 minute. Pour this into your serving jug and half-fill with blueberry and mint ice cubes. Top with the prosecco and stir well. Place a few more blueberry and mint ice cubes into the serving glasses. Pour the drink into the glasses and garnish each one with a blueberry skewer.

STRAWBERRY AND JASMINE ICED TEA

Goji berries are something you should try to consume everyday. They are high in antioxidants, vitamins C and A, fibre, and iron. I can't think of a better way to get your daily dose than in this refreshing drink! The delicate but exotic scent of jasmine pairs so well with the fresh strawberries and basil.

SERVES 2
1 tablespoon goji berries • 1 jasmine teabag (I use Tea Pigs)
6 strawberries, hulled and quartered • 6 fresh basil leaves
80ml goji berry liqueur • 40ml Bacardi white rum
10ml Mandarine Napoléon • Ice cubes or
Strawberry Ice Cubes (see page 12)
Extra strawberries, basil leaves and edible jasmine flowers
(optional), to garnish

EQUIPMENT
Cocktail shaker, Muddler, Cocktail stirrer
and 2 tall glasses

Pour 200ml boiling water over the goji berries and teabag. Leave to steep and cool.

Put the strawberries, basil and goji liqueur in the bottom of the cocktail shaker and muddle until the strawberries have turned into a pulp. Add the rum, Mandarine Napoléon and a handful of ice cubes. Put the top of the cocktail shaker on and shake for 15 seconds.

Fill the glasses with strawberry ice cubes and pour over the cocktail mixture. Top up with the jasmine tea, including all the goji berries. Garnish with halved strawberries, a few basil leaves and a jasmine flower (optional).

KOMBUCHA PIMMS PUNCH

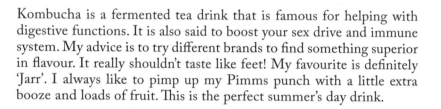

Kombucha is a fermented tea drink that is famous for helping with digestive functions. It is also said to boost your sex drive and immune system. My advice is to try different brands to find something superior in flavour. It really shouldn't taste like feet! My favourite is definitely 'Jarr'. I always like to pimp up my Pimms punch with a little extra booze and loads of fruit. This is the perfect summer's day drink.

SERVES 4
Ice cubes or Mint Ice Cubes (see page 12)
150ml Pimms · 50ml Cointreau · 50ml citron vodka
12 fresh mint leaves · 1 unwaxed lime, sliced
1 unwaxed orange, sliced · 6 strawberries, halved
¼ cucumber, sliced · 1 peach, cut into wedges
470ml 'Jarr' original organic kombucha
150ml soda water

EQUIPMENT
Large jug and 4 serving glasses

Grab a jug and fill it halfway up with ice cubes or mint ice cubes. Pour over the Pimms, Cointreau and citron vodka and stir well. Add the mint, prepared fruit, 2 handfuls of ice, the kombucha and soda water. Stir well and serve.

POMEGRANATE AND VANILLA COSMO

Pomegranates are particularly high in vitamin C and antioxidants. They are also said to curb your hunger and protect you from disease. Always use a 100% pomegranate juice with no added sugar. Or even better, blend seeds from 2 pomeganates with a little water and strain to get pure juice. The tangy taste makes it the perfect match for a Cosmopolitan cocktail.

SERVES 4
Ice cubes • 75ml citron vodka
25ml Cointreau • 200ml pomegranate juice
15ml agave nectar• Seeds from ½ vanilla pod
Orange curls, vanilla pods and pomegranate seeds, to garnish

EQUIPMENT
Cocktail shaker, Cocktail strainer and 2 Martini glasses

Half-fill a cocktail shaker with ice and pour in the vodka, Cointreau, pomegranate juice, agave nectar and vanilla seeds. Pop the lid on the shaker and shake vigorously for 1 minute. Strain into chilled glasses. Garnish with curled orange rind, vanilla pods and pomegranate seeds.

THYME BRAMBLE

This is a quintessential British cocktail usually made with crème de mure, gin and lemon. My version takes away the crème de mure and exchanges it for a homemade blackberry syrup that doesn't contain any sugar. The flavour of both the blackberries and lemon thyme really shine through. I've also added a little acai for a great superfood kick, but it's optional.

SERVES 2

60g sweet blackberries, halved · 2 tablespoons agave nectar
4 sprigs of lemon thyme
1 teaspoon acai powder (optional) · 80ml gin
20ml lemon juice · Crushed ice
Frozen skewered blackberries and lemon thyme
sprigs, to garnish

EQUIPMENT

Small saucepan, Cocktail strainer, Cocktail shaker
and 2 short tumbler glasses

Place the blackberries, agave nectar, lemon thyme and 150ml water into a small saucepan. Bring it up to a boil, then reduce the heat and allow to simmer for 10 minutes. Remove from the heat, stir through the acai powder and leave to cool. Pass the mixture through a fine strainer and add it to a cocktail shaker along with a handful of crushed ice, the gin and lemon juice. Place the top of the shaker on and shake for 30 seconds.

Fill the glasses with crushed ice. Strain the drink over the ice. Top with another handful of crushed ice and garnish with a sprig of lemon thyme and a frozen blackberry skewer.

PINK CHAMPAGNE AND GOJI POPSICLES

Not all cocktails need to be enjoyed in a glass. These popsicles are the perfect way to cool down on a hot summer's day. Filled with fruit, goji berries and pink champagne, they make the perfect adult icy treat!

MAKES 8
1 tablespoon goji berries · 150g mixed berries
16 small, fresh mint leaves · 400ml pink champagne
20ml goji liqueur · 20ml Cointreau
Crushed ice · Extra berries and mint leaves, to garnish

EQUIPMENT
8-mould ice lolly tray and wooden
popsicle sticks · Jug

Pour a small amount of boiling water over the goji berries and leave to soak for 5 minutes, then drain.

Fill the popsicle moulds with a mixture of berries, goji berries and mint leaves.

Pour the pink champagne, goji liqueur and Cointreau into a jug and stir gently. Fill each mould with the mixture. Place the lids on and insert a popsicle stick into each. Place in the freezer overnight or until completely frozen.

Pour a little warm water over the moulds to loosen them and serve the popsicles on a tray of crushed ice, sprinkled with mint leaves and berries.

DRINK YOUR GREENS

Pea Cooler

G & Tea Heaven

Genmaicha Goodness

Kale and Pineapple Daiquiri

Apple Cider-tini

Papaya the Sailorman, Toot! Toot!

Green Goddess Smoothie

Grass is Always Greener

Cucumber Martini

PEA COOLER

The humble pea… It's a celebrated green here in Britain and, I, for one love the sweet little things! They are full of antioxidants and vitamins, and are known to improve heart health. They are high in protein and can even boost your immune system. Their sweet flavour matches so well with lemon and elderflower. St Germain is an amazing elderflower liqueur, so give it a try.

SERVES 2
50g cooked peas · 20ml agave nectar
100ml fresh cucumber juice (from approx. ½ cucumber)
30ml lemon juice · 1 sprig of tarragon · 50ml vodka
50ml St Germain · Ice cubes · Peas in their pods,
pea sprouts and thin cucumber slices, to garnish

EQUIPMENT
Cocktail shaker, Muddler, Cocktail strainer
and 2 coupe glasses

Place the peas and agave nectar into a cocktail shaker and muddle well for 1 minute. You want to extract as much pea flavour and juice as possible. Pour in the cucumber juice, lemon juice, tarragon, vodka and St Germain. Half-fill the cocktail shaker with ice cubes and replace the top. Shake vigorously for 1 minute. Strain into the glasses, making sure to get a nice layer of froth in each glass. Garnish with an opened pea pod, pea sprouts and cucumber slices.

G & TEA HEAVEN

This is a healthy spin on my all-time favourite drink, the gin and tonic. I've used green tea as the base because it's packed with antioxidants and nutrients. It can improve brain function and aid fat loss – a cocktail that makes you smarter and lose weight you say!?! #winning

SERVES 2

1 tablespoon organic green tea leaves
Juice and zest of 1 unwaxed lime
Juice and zest of ½ unwaxed lemon
2 tablespoons agave nectar • Ice
cubes • 80ml gin • Soda water
4 lime wedges, to garnish

EQUIPMENT

Small saucepan, Cocktail shaker,
Tea strainer, Cocktail strainer
and 2 highball glasses

Add the tea leaves, lime juice and zest, lemon juice and zest, agave nectar and 150ml water to a small saucepan. Bring to a simmer, then reduce the heat and allow to gently simmer for 5 minutes. Leave to cool.

Half-fill a cocktail shaker with ice cubes. Strain the tea mixture into the shaker and add the gin. Place the lid on and shake for 10 seconds. Fill the glasses with ice and strain the mixture over. Top with soda water and garnish with squeezed lime wedges.

GENMAICHA GOODNESS

Genmaicha is a special blend of Japanese green tea and roasted brown rice. It has a delicious roasted nutty aroma and is rich in antioxidants. I've paired it with the Japanese flavours of yuzu and saké to create a lovely mellow drink.

SERVES 2

1 heaped tablespoon genmaicha tea
leaves •250ml boiling water
2 tablespoons honey • 15ml yuzu
juice • 40ml saké • 25ml Cointreau
25ml vodka • Ice cubes
Edible orchids, to garnish

EQUIPMENT

Small saucepan, Cocktail shaker, Tea
strainer, Cocktail stirrer and
2 highball glasses

Place the tea into a saucepan and pour over the boiling water. Stir through the honey and leave the mixture to infuse and cool down completely.

Strain the mixture into a cocktail shaker and stir through the yuzu, saké, Cointreau and vodka. Fill each glass with ice cubes and divide the mixture between the glasses. Top with a few more ice cubes and garnish with a couple of edible orchids.

KALE AND PINEAPPLE DAIQUIRI

Kale is one of the most nutrient-dense foods on the planet! It's packed with powerful antioxidants, and vitamins C and K. It's quite difficult to break down and it doesn't juice well, so blending is the best way to get the most nutrients from it. Made with pineapple, apple and fresh mint, getting your buzz on while drinking your greens has never tasted so good!

SERVES 2
40ml Bacardi white rum · 40ml Ciroc apple vodka
70ml fresh Granny Smith apple juice
1 handful of kale leaves
50g frozen pineapple (2cm chunks)
6 small, fresh mint leaves · 250g crushed ice
Pineapple spears and pineapple wedges, to garnish

EQUIPMENT
High-speed blender and
2 Martini glasses

Place the rum, apple vodka, apple juice, kale, frozen pineapple and mint into a high-speed blender. Blend for 1 minute, or until completely smooth. This can take longer depending on your blender. Next, add the crushed ice and blend to a slushy consistency. Pour into the glasses and garnish each one with a pineapple spear and a wedge of pineapple.

APPLE CIDER-TINI

Organic apple cider vinegar is anti-bacterial and can even cure a sore throat. It contains potassium and enzymes that can also help with that tired feeling. I have a shot most mornings! It tastes delicious and it feels invigorating. This is my spin on the Appletini...

SERVES 2

Ice cubes · 80ml vodka (I use Absolut) · 25ml organic apple cider vinegar · 160ml fresh Granny Smith apple juice 10ml agave nectar · 6 dashes peach bitters 2 thin slices of Granny Smith apple, to garnish

EQUIPMENT

Cocktail shaker, Cocktail strainer and 2 large Martini glasses

Half-fill a cocktail shaker with ice cubes. Pour in the vodka, vinegar, apple juice, agave nectar and bitters. Place the lid on and shake vigorously for 1 minute. Remove the lid and strain into the glasses.

Cut a small slit into each piece of sliced apple, using a sharp knife, and place onto the side of each glass to garnish.

PAPAYA THE SAILORMAN TOOT! TOOT!

I couldn't resist the title for this one. The two main ingredients are so good for you! Papaya is high in vitamin C and is great for digestion and your immune system. And spinach… well we all know what spinach is good for – it's a nutritional powerhouse – just look at the guns on Popeye!

SERVES 2
70ml Havana 8-year-old rum • 1 large handful of spinach leaves
200g frozen papaya • 100ml coconut water
1 tablespoon coconut palm sugar • 100g ice cubes
Wedges of papaya and orange edible flowers, to garnish

EQUIPMENT
High-speed blender and 2 short glasses

Place the rum, spinach, frozen papaya, coconut water, coconut palm sugar and ice cubes into a high-speed blender. Blend until smooth. Add a few ice cubes to each glass and pour over the drink. Garnish with a wedge of papaya and some edible flowers.

GREEN GODDESS SMOOTHIE

This healthy smoothie is full of greens so will boost your entire system with a multitude of nutrients, vitamins and antioxidants. The blending process breaks everything down for easy digestion. The avocado gives it a lovely creaminess and the frozen fruit adds natural sweetness. No-one need ever know that this is a cocktail!

SERVES 2
200ml fresh Granny Smith apple juice • 70ml fresh
cucumber juice (approx ½ cucumber) • 1 handful of kale
1 handful of spinach • 80g avocado flesh
20 small, fresh mint leaves • 150g frozen kiwi fruit
100g frozen grapes • 70ml coconut water
150g ice cubes • 80ml vodka (I use Chase)
Frozen sliced kiwi fruit and grapes, to garnish

EQUIPMENT
High-speed blender, 2 straws
and 2 tall smoothie glasses

Place all the ingredients into a high-speed blender and blend until smooth. Pour into the glasses and garnish with sliced frozen grapes and small frozen kiwi chunks. Could it be any simpler?!

GRASS IS ALWAYS GREENER

A cocktail that helps your liver?! Wheatgrass is 70% chlorophyll, which helps purify your liver and neutralise toxins within your body. It contains essential vitamins, minerals and amino acids, so is a natural healer. 50ml of wheatgrass is equivalent to eating nearly 700g green leafy vegetables. Go for the fresh or frozen wheatgrass juice for more nutrients and a much better flavour. You can get it from health-food stores or order it online.

SERVES 2
80ml vodka (I use Zubrowka) • 100ml fresh Pink Lady apple juice
50ml fresh/frozen wheatgrass juice
1 kiwi fruit, peeled and roughly chopped
120g fresh pineapple chunks
2 sprigs of tarragon, leaves only • 100g ice cubes
2 oversized ice cubes • Tarragon sprigs, to garnish

EQUIPMENT
High-speed blender and 2 short tumblers

Add the vodka, apple juice, wheatgrass juice, kiwi fruit, pineapple, tarragon and ice cubes into a high-speed blender. Blend until smooth. Place an oversized ice cube into each glass and pour the cocktail over the ice. Garnish with a tarragon sprig in each glass.

CUCUMBER MARTINI

Cucumbers are a great source of vitamins A and K and dietary fibre. They have the highest water content of any solid food, so this Martini is sure to keep you hydrated. Hendricks gin is infused with cucumber and rose, which makes it the perfect match for this refreshing tipple.

SERVES 2
100ml Hendricks gin • 100ml fresh cucumber juice (approx ½ cucumber) • 30ml Martini Bianco • 6 large fresh mint leaves
4–5 drops rosewater • Ice cubes
2 thick slices of cucumber, sliced at an angle

EQUIPMENT
Cocktail shaker, Cocktail strainer
and 2 large Martini glasses

Half-fill a cocktail shaker with ice. Add the gin, cucumber juice, Martini Bianco, mint leaves and rosewater. Place the lid on and shake vigorously for 1 minute. Remove the lid and strain the liquid into the glasses. Add a thick slice of cucumber to each and serve.

TOTALLY TROPICAL

Passion Mango Margarita

Watermelon, Rose and Mint Mojito

Kefir Mango Lassi

Kiwi and Strawberry Daiquiri

Rum Punch

Chocolates for My Date

Cacao and Avocado Popsicles

Hemp Piña Colada

Monkey Nuts

PASSION MANGO MARGARITA

♀ ♀

Mangoes are super-sweet and so damn good for you. They are great for your skin and they can help reduce cholesterol and alkalise your body. Passion fruit are also very high in vitamin C, minerals and fibre. These two are the ideal flavour combo for a bangin' Margarita. Get involved!

SERVES 2

25ml passion fruit juice · 75ml tequila (I use AquaRiva Blanco)
30ml Cointreau · Juice of ½ lime
100g frozen ripe mango chunks · 25ml agave nectar
Crushed ice · 50g Maldon sea salt
Zest of 1 unwaxed lime · Extra passion fruit halves, to garnish

EQUIPMENT
Strainer, High-speed blender and 2 coupe glasses

Prepare the passion fruit juice by scooping out the flesh from 2-3 large ripe passion fruit. Place the pulp into a strainer and press out all the juice using the back of a spoon. You should end up with 25ml.

Add this to a high-speed blender along with the tequila, Cointreau, lime juice, frozen mango, agave nectar and a small handful of crushed ice. Blend for about 1 minute, or until smooth.

Mix together the sea salt and lime zest and tip onto a small side plate. Wet the rims of the serving glasses with a little lime juice and tip the glasses upside-down onto the salt. Spin the glasses until you have an even rim of lime salt.

Fill the glasses three-quarters full with crushed ice. Pour over the margarita and garnish with half a passion fruit.

WATERMELON, ROSE AND MINT MOJITO

Watermelon is just great for hydration and each sip of this will fill you with vitamins A, B6 and C. It contains electrolytes too, which prevent dehydration – perfect, really, for a fresh and cooling drink with just a hint of rose.

SERVES 2
150g watermelon chunks • 12 fresh mint leaves
2 teaspoons agave nectar • 2 teaspoons lime juice
6 drops rosewater • Crushed ice
80ml dark rum (I use Havana Club)
Extra diced watermelon chunks, lime wedges, watermelon wedges
and pink rose petals (optional), to garnish

EQUIPMENT
Muddler, Cocktail stirrer and
2 tall glasses

Divide the watermelon, mint, agave nectar, lime juice and rosewater between 2 tall glasses. Muddle well until all the juice is released from the watermelon. Fill each glass with crushed ice and add 40ml rum to each glass. Stir well and garnish with a few diced watermelon chunks, lime wedges, watermelon wedges and optional pink rose petals.

KEFIR MANGO LASSI

For those of you that haven't heard of kefir, it's simply a fermented milk. It contains more powerful healthy probiotics than yogurt, which are very helpful for digestion and gut health. It has a lovely tang to it and works brilliantly in this traditional Indian drink.

SERVES 2

1 pinch of good-quality saffron • 1 teaspoon tamarind paste
2 tablespoon honey • $\frac{1}{4}$ teaspoon fresh ground cardamom
10g whole pistachios
350ml organic kefir cultured milk
150g ice cubes • 160g frozen ripe mango
70ml dark rum • Extra saffron, chopped pistachios
and dried rose petals, to garnish

EQUIPMENT
High-speed blender and 2 serving glasses

Steep the saffron in 1 tablespoon of boiling water for about 5 minutes to release its colour and flavour. Add this to a high-speed blender along with the tamarind paste, honey, ground cardamom, pistachios and kefir. Leave the mixture to stand for 5 minutes – this really helps with intensifying the saffron flavour. Blend for 30 seconds. This gives the honey a chance to mix well with the ingredients first before the cold ingredients are added.

Next add the ice, mango and rum to the blender. Blend again for 1 minute, or until smooth. Pour into the glasses and garnish with a few extra saffron strands, chopped pistachios and rose petals.

KIWI AND STRAWBERRY DAIQUIRI

Kiwi fruit have such a unique flavour, I just love them. They also contain phyto-nutrients and more vitamin C than an orange. I love freezing fruit for cocktails because it gives you the most amazing consistency. Strawberries are also a great source of vitamin C and antioxidants, so basically, this drink is both delicious and nutritious!

SERVES 2
160g frozen strawberries
60g frozen kiwi fruit
10ml lime juice • 70ml coconut water
150g ice cubes • 2 tablespoons agave
nectar • 6 fresh mint leaves • 80ml
Bacardi white rum • Peeled and sliced
kiwi fruit, strawberries and edible
flowers, to garnish

EQUIPMENT
High-speed blender and
2 tall coupe glasses

Place the frozen strawberries, frozen kiwi, lime juice, coconut water, ice cubes, agave nectar, mint and rum into a high-speed blender and blend until smooth.

Pour into the glasses and garnish with kiwi slices, halved strawberries and edible flowers.

RUM PUNCH

The classic Jamaican Rum Punch is a fruity mixture of orange juice, pineapple juice, white rum and grenadine syrup. A very sweet tipple that, in the past, has given me one of the worst hangovers ever experienced! This much cleaner version uses fresh fruit and vegetable juices, so it will save you from that horrible sugar-filled headache the next morning.

SERVES 2
80ml dark rum • 100ml fresh orange
juice • 50ml carrot juice
120g fresh pineapple chunks
100ml coconut water • Ice cubes
2 teaspoons beetroot juice • Fresh
mint leaves, cherries and orange
slices, to garnish

EQUIPMENT
High-speed blender and
2 punch glasses

Add the rum, orange juice, carrot juice, pineapple chunks, coconut water and a few ice cubes into a high-speed blender. Blend for 1 minute, or until completely smooth.

Half-fill the glasses with ice cubes and pour the mixture over. Using a small teaspoon, gently pour a little beetroot juice around the edge of each glass. Garnish with mint leaves, cherries and orange slices.

CHOCOLATES FOR MY DATE

I wanted to create an adult 'hard shake' that's packed with energy and flavour. I've used the sweetness from dates, pineapple and banana along with the energy from raw cacao, guarana and hemp seeds.

SERVES 2
50g medjool dates, roughly chopped
30g raw cacao powder · 80ml dark rum
200ml coconut milk drink (I use Coco)
3 teaspoons date syrup (or maple syrup) · 60g frozen banana
chunks · 50g frozen pineapple chunks
2 teaspoons hemp seeds · 30g toasted hazelnuts
1 teaspoon guarana powder · 150g crushed ice
Extra crushed ice, to fill the glasses · Extra cocoa nibs, medjool
dates and chopped toasted hazelnuts, to garnish

EQUIPMENT
High-speed blender, Straws and 2 tall glasses

Place all the ingredients into a high-speed blender and blend for at least 1 minute, or until completely smooth.

Pour into the glasses and garnish with a sprinkle of cacao nibs and chopped toasted hazelnuts. Make a small slit in the medjool date and press down onto the side of each glass.

CACAO AND AVOCADO POPSICLES

Avocadoes are loaded with nutrients and antioxidants. They are packed with potassium, vitamin E and iron. These popsicles are a revelation and great for a dinner party – sweet and rum-filled with little bites of cacao nibs for crunch. Experiment if you like… add your favourite dried fruit or chopped nuts for a delightful change.

MAKES 8
250g avocado flesh · 50g raw cacao powder
100ml maple syrup · 300ml unsweetened almond milk
Seeds from 1 vanilla pod · 125ml rum (I use Sailor Jerry's)
25g cacao nibs · 80g dark chocolate, nibbed pistachios
and cacao nibs, to garnish

EQUIPMENT
High-speed blender or food processor,
8-mould ice lolly tray and wooden popsicle sticks

Place the avocado flesh, cacao, maple syrup, almond milk, vanilla seeds and rum into a high-speed blender and blend until smooth. Stir through the cacao nibs and pour the mixture into the moulds. Place the lids on and insert a popsicle stick into each. Freeze for a minimum of 3 hours or overnight.

If you want to keep the sugar out, eat them the way they are. But if you want to add a little chocolate into the mix, melt 80g dark chocolate and leave to cool. Remove each popsicle from their mould, place on a tray lined with baking parchment and drizzle with the melted dark chocolate. Sprinkle with some chopped pistachios and cacao nibs. Return to the freezer for 20 minutes or so to set. Serve when ready.

HEMP PIÑA COLADA

Now I couldn't write a cocktail book without including a cheeky Piña Colada – it's a bit of a guilty pleasure of mine! This version is made with ripe, fresh pineapple chunks and the mild nutty flavour of hemp seeds. If you didn't know, hemp seeds are one of the most nutrient-dense seeds in the world. I say sprinkle those bad boys everywhere!

SERVES 2
100ml white rum (I use Bacardi) • 50ml coconut water
60ml coconut cream • 200g fresh, ripe pineapple chunks
100g ice cubes • 10ml lime juice
30ml agave nectar • 2 teaspoons hemp seeds
Coconut Water Ice Cubes (see page 12)
Pineapple wedges, lime wedges and hemp
seeds, to sprinkle

EQUIPMENT
High-speed blender, 2 tall glasses, Straws,
Pink flamingo stirrers and Cocktail umbrellas

Place the rum, coconut water, coconut cream, pineapple, ice cubes, lime juice, agave nectar and hemp seeds in a high-speed blender and blend until smooth.

Fill the glasses with coconut water ice cubes and pour over the Piña Colada mixture. Garnish with pineapple wedges, lime wedges and a sprinkle of hemp seeds. Go mad with straws, colourful stirrers and cocktail umbrellas, and imagine you're lying on the beach in Barbados.

MONKEY NUTS

Bananas and nuts make the most awesome flavour combo and are packed with energy, good fats and nutrients. I've teamed these babies up with the Peruvian superfood energy of maca powder. Maca is said to increase your libido and can help with endurance. It can also help with improving your mood. #boom

SERVES 2
100g frozen ripe banana chunks
2 teaspoons maca powder • 80ml Jack Daniel's
200ml almond milk • 2 tablespoons organic 3-nut butter or
peanut butter • 2 teaspoons maple syrup • Seeds from 1 vanilla
pod • 200g crushed ice • Extra sliced banana, vanilla pods
and toasted chopped nuts (optional), to garnish

EQUIPMENT
High-speed blender, Straws and
2 drinking jars

Place all the ingredients in a high-speed blender and blend until smooth. Pour into jars and top with the crushed ice. Garnish with sliced banana and halved vanilla pods. And maybe some crushed toasted nuts too!

SMOKEY, SPICY, SOUR, SEXY

Blood Orange and Carrot Negroni

Dark 'n' Scoby

Yuzu Gunshot Margarita

Indian Summer

Some Like it Bloody Hot

Ginseng Hot Toddy

Get Your Buzz On!

Pear and Cinnamon Sour

Baobab Beetroot Sherbet

Juicy Penicillin

Pineapple and Pink Peppercorn Mulled Wine

BLOOD ORANGE AND CARROT NEGRONI

I'm a big lover of a Negroni, but I sometimes like to make mine with Aperol so it's not as bitter as the original. If you aren't using Antica Formula as your choice of red vermouth, definitely give Aperol a try. I wouldn't dream of making a Negroni without it. With added carrot juice and blood orange juice, this drink is just perfection.

SERVES 2
2 thick slices of blood orange • 1 teaspoon coconut palm sugar
Ice cubes • 50ml Aperol • 50ml Antica Formula • 50ml Bombay
Sapphire or Tanqueray gin • 50ml carrot juice • 50ml blood
orange juice • 2 oversized square ice cubes
1 baby heritage carrot, halved lengthways

EQUIPMENT
Blow torch, Cocktail shaker and
2 short tumblers

Prepare the garnish by sprinkling each slice of blood orange with the coconut palm sugar. Run a blow torch over each one until the sugar melts and caramelises. Set aside.

Throw a handful of ice into a cocktail shaker. Pour in the Aperol, Antica Formula, gin, carrot juice and blood orange juice. Give it 3-4 shakes.

Place an oversized ice cube in each glass. These cubes are much better for drinks like this because they melt at a slower rate than normal-sized ice cubes. The last thing you want is a watered-down Negroni! Strain the contents of the shaker into the glasses.

Garnish by skewering one piece of carrot through the orange slice. Lay this in the glass so that the orange is floating. If you can, sip a little of the drink through the caramelised piece of orange… Ahh heaven!

DARK 'N' SCOBY

SCOBY is the acronym for Symbiotic Culture Of Bacteria and Yeast. The Scoby is the culture that ferments the tea and turns it into kombucha. This is my version of a Dark 'n' Stormy using a delicious ginger kombucha. This drink has spice, tang and fizz. And it's pretty damn good for you too. I could drink it all day long…

SERVES 2
6 thin slices of ginger • 1 lime, quartered
4 lime leaves • 30ml agave nectar • Crushed ice
470ml 'Jarr' organic ginger kombucha
100ml rum (I use Gosling Black)
Extra limes leaves and lime wedges, to garnish

EQUIPMENT
Muddler, Straws and 2 serving glasses

Divide the ginger, lime, lime leaves and agave nectar between the glasses and muddle well until all the lime juice and flavours from the ginger and lime leaves have been extracted.

Fill each glass to the top with crushed ice and place a straw in each glass. Divide the kombucha between the glasses. Place a large spoon upside down with the tip touching the inside of the glass and float the rum on top by pouring it gently over the spoon.

Garnish with a few extra lime leaves and lime wedges.

YUZU GUNSHOT MARGARITA

Yuzu is one of my all-time favourite flavours. It's super-intense and somewhere between a grapefruit, lime and Amalfi lemon. If you like drinks with zing, this one is for you. I've paired this up with mezcal because its smokiness goes so well with yuzu. Frozen grapes and green tea mean you'll get your daily does of antioxidants too. What more could you want?

SERVES 2
100ml mezcal (I use Quiquiriqui) · 300g ice cubes
200g frozen white grapes · 30ml yuzu juice
100ml cold green tea · 40ml agave nectar
50g Maldon sea salt · Zest of 1 unwaxed lime
Frozen grape skewers, to garnish

EQUIPMENT
High-speed blender and 2 short tumblers

Place the mezcal, ice cubes, frozen grapes, yuzu juice, green tea and agave nectar into a high-speed blender and blend until smooth.

Next, mix the sea salt together with the lime zest and tip it out onto a small side plate. Cut the lime you used for the zest and rub the rims of the serving glasses with a little lime juice. Tip the glasses upside-down onto the salt and spin the glass until you have an even rim of lime salt. Pour the icy cocktail into glasses and garnish with a frozen grape skewer.

INDIAN SUMMER

The good news is that fresh turmeric contains strong medicinal qualities; it's anti-inflammatory and can also increase the antioxidant capacity in your body. The not-so-good news is that it stains the crap out of everything! So just be prepared, wear gloves and have some hot soapy water ready to clean your juicer too.

SERVES 2
40g fresh turmeric root (20ml turmeric juice)
10 cardamom pods, lightly crushed • 2 tablespoons agave nectar
Coriander stalks, chopped, from a 30g bunch
1 unwaxed lime • Ice cubes • 80ml gin (I use Bombay)
150ml sparkling water • Fresh coriander leaves, to garnish

EQUIPMENT
Electric juicer, Small saucepan, Cocktail strainer
and 2 tall glasses

Put the turmeric root through an electric juicer – you want 20ml in total. Place the juice into a small saucepan along with the cardamom, agave nectar and coriander stalks (give these a bit of a bash with a rolling pin to release some juice). Peel the lime zest off the lime and add it to the pan along with 200ml water. Place onto the heat. Bring up to the boil, reduce the heat and allow the liquid to simmer gently for 10-15 minutes, or until it has reduced by half. Squeeze the juice from the lime into the saucepan and leave to cool.

Strain the mixture. Fill the glasses with ice and divide the turmeric infusion between the glasses. Add 40ml of gin to each glass and stir well. Top the glasses with sparkling water and garnish with coriander leaves.

SOME LIKE IT BLOODY HOT

This is my version of a Thai-inspired Bloody Mary. I adore chilli and I like my Bloody Marys bloody hot. Chillies are great as they stimulate your appetite and your digestion. If you don't like things spicy, I would omit the Sriracha altogether or chose the less-hot version.

SERVES 2

2 lemongrass stalks, bashed with the back of a knife and cut in half
½ small red bird's eye chilli, cut lengthways · 4 lime leaves,
lightly crushed · 1 teaspoon grated fresh ginger · 2 tablespoons
agave nectar · Ice cubes · 80ml vodka (I use Absolut) · 8 Thai
basil leaves · 1 tablespoon lime juice
2 teaspoons soy sauce · ¼-½ teaspoon Sriracha 'Super Hot'
chilli sauce · 200ml tomato juice · Ice cubes
Extra lime wedges, limes leaves, 1 lemongrass stalk (halved
lengthways) and Thai basil leaves, to garnish

EQUIPMENT
Small saucepan, Fine-mesh sieve, Cocktail shaker
and 2 tall glasses

Place the lemongrass, chilli, lime leaves, ginger, agave nectar and 200ml water into a small saucepan. Bring to the boil, then simmer for about 10 minutes, or until the liquid reduces by half. Leave to cool. Strain the liquid through a fine-mesh sieve.

Fill a cocktail shaker half-full of ice cubes, pour the strained liquid in along with the vodka, Thai basil leaves, lime juice, soy sauce, sriracha and tomato juice. Shake vigorously for 1 minute to extract as much flavour as possible from the Thai basil leaves. Fill the glasses with ice cubes and strain the drink into each glass. Garnish with a lime wedge, lime leaves, lemongrass and Thai basil.

GINSENG HOT TODDY

Warming, spiced, whisky-spiked drinks on a cold winter's night can really comfort the soul. Ginger is great for digestion, has strong, flu-fighting qualities and can reduce blood pressure. Ginseng helps with energy and cognitive function, and there's lots of vitamin C in the mix with both orange and lemon juices.

SERVES 2
1 chamomile teabag
4 thick slices of fresh ginger, lightly scored
4 strips of orange peel • 120ml orange juice
25ml lemon juice • 5 cloves
6 cardamom pods, lightly bashed • 2 star anise
4 pieces of dried ginseng • 2 tablespoons honey
80ml whisky • 6 dashes orange bitters

EQUIPMENT
Small saucepan and 2 heatproof glasses or mugs

Place the teabag into 250ml boiling water and leave to steep for 5 minutes, then remove the teabag.

Place the remaining ingredients into a small saucepan. Add the chamomile tea. Bring the mixture up to a gentle simmer. Cook on a very low simmer for 10 minutes to allow the flavours to infuse.

Serve in heatproof glasses or mugs, sit back and relax…

GET YOUR BUZZ ON!

My version of an energy-packed Espresso Martini with the added buzz of guarana. You can use vodka but do give tequila a try. It really does work so well with coffee – I just love it! A good friend, Craig, urged me to try it quite a few years ago, in a swanky rooftop bar in Melbourne and I have been a convert ever since.

SERVES 2
80ml gold tequila
200ml cooled espresso coffee
20ml amaretto · 30ml agave nectar
or maple syrup · 20ml Cointreau
½ teaspoon guarana powder
Ice cubes · Espresso beans,
to garnish

EQUIPMENT
Large metal cocktail shaker,
Strainer and 2 chilled coupe glasses

Place the tequila, espresso, amaretto, agave nectar, Cointreau and guarana powder into a cocktail shaker. Add in 2 handfuls of ice cubes. Shake vigorously for 1-2 minutes. The more you shake, the better the froth will be.

Pour through the pourer or strainer into the glasses. Garnish each with 3 espresso beans. Heaven!

PEAR AND CINNAMON SOUR

I do love a sour! That perfect balance between sweet and tangy. The possibilities are endless as far as flavours go, but I've decided to stick with something I know works well. I do hope you agree…

SERVES 2
120ml pear juice · 80ml lemon juice
1 large egg white · 80ml amaretto
2 pinches of ground cinnamon
Ice cubes · Angostura Bitters
Pear wedges · Cinnamon sticks and
ground cinnamon, to garnish

EQUIPMENT
Large metal cocktail shaker, Strainer
and 2 tumbler glasses

Place the pear juice, lemon juice, egg white, amaretto and ground cinnamon into a cocktail shaker with 2 handfuls of ice cubes. Shake vigorously for 1-2 minutes. The more you shake, the better the froth!

Put a few ice cubes into each glass and pour the sour through the strainer so that you retain as much foam as possible. Garnish with a pear wedge (make a little incision on the skin side and secure it to the side of the glass). Pop in a cinnamon stick and add a few drops of Angostura Bitters on top of the froth. Sprinkle the pear with a bit of cinnamon and enjoy.

BAOBAB BEETROOT SHERBET

I nicknamed one of my favourite juice combinations Beetroot Sherbet a while back. It has the earthy flavour of beetroot, but with the most delicious citrus sherbet tang! Beetroot is an excellent source of folic acid and fibre and is also known to improve stamina. Gram for gram, baobab contains more vitamin C than oranges, more calcium than milk and more iron than meat, so it's definitely something worth using!

SERVES 2
1 beetroot · 1 pink grapefruit, peeled
1 large orange, peeled · ½ Amalfi lemon, peeled
2 large carrots · 80ml citron vodka · 10ml agave nectar
2 teaspoons baobab powder · Ice cubes · Beetroot juice ice
cubes (see page 12) · Frozen blueberry skewers, to garnish

EQUIPMENT
Electric juicer, Cocktail shaker, Cocktail stirrer and 2 tall glasses

Due to the fact that I don't usually make this juice by meaurements (ml) – this one is written a little differently. Put the beetroot, pink grapefruit, orange, lemon and carrots through an electric juicer.

Pour half of this juice into a cocktail shaker along with the vodka, agave nectar and baobab powder. Add a handful of ice cubes and shake vigorously for 30 seconds – you want to make sure the baobab powder has distributed itself well, with no lumps!

Pour the rest of the juice into the shaker – if it's big enough. Stir well with the cocktail stirrer. Fill the glasses with beetroot juice ice cubes and using the pourer of the shaker, divide the drink between the two glasses. Garnish with a frozen blueberry skewer.

JUICY PENICILLIN

Quite a few of the ingredients in this drink have great flu-busting qualities and contain loads of vitamin C. Honey and apple cider vinegar soothe the throat, and echinacea strengthens your immune system. Just what the doctor ordered!

SERVES 2
80ml whisky · 3 tablespoons clear honey
200ml orange juice · 20ml lemon juice
20ml organic apple cider vinegar
6 dashes Angostura Bitters
12 drops echinacea tincture (liquid echinacea)
Ice cubes · Bee pollen, orange skin curls
and natural honeycomb, to garnish

EQUIPMENT
Cocktail shaker, Cocktail stirrer
and 2 short glasses

Pour the whisky into a cocktail shaker and stir in the honey until it has all incorporated. Next, add the orange juice, lemon juice, apple cider vinegar, Angostura Bitters and echinacea. Stir well.

Fill the glasses with ice cubes and pour over the penicillin. Garnish with an orange curl, a sprinkle of bee pollen and a nice piece of natural honeycomb.

PINEAPPLE AND PINK PEPPERCORN MULLED WINE

I love spiced mulled wine! Especially when there are chunks of spiced and wine-soaked fruit to enjoy too. Experiment with your favourite fruit – stone fruit also work really well.

SERVES 4
750ml Rioja (red wine) · 100g diced pineapple
4 tablespoons coconut palm sugar · 4 star anise
2 large cinnamom sticks · 10 black peppercorns
4 cardamon pods, crushed · 10 Szechuan peppercorns
½ teaspoon pink peppercorns · 6 cloves
200ml orange or clementine juice
Sliced orange/clementine, cinnamon sticks
and pink peppercorns, to garnish

EQUIPMENT
Medium saucepan, Muslin, Serving jug
and 4 heatproof glasses

Pour the Rioja into a saucepan and add the pineapple, coconut sugar, star anise and cinnamon sticks.

Cut a small square of muslin and place the black peppercorns, cardamom pods, Szechuan peppercorns, pink peppercorns and cloves in the centre of the cloth. Tie up with a piece of string and add to the saucepan. Place on a medium heat and bring up to a low simmer then leave to simmer gently for 15 minutes. Remove from the heat and stir through the orange or clementine juice.

Divide between the glasses, add a slice of orange or clementine to each. Add half a cinnamon stick and one star anise to each glass. Sprinkle with pink peppercorns and serve.

INDEX

THANK YOUS

Firstly I have to thank the lovely Sophie Allen. If it wasn't for you and that slightly tipsy evening we spent together, talking about the idea, this book would never have happened. Thank you for having the foresight to ask me. It was such a brilliantly open and creative process for me and I'm so grateful that you and Kyle believed in me.

My next thank you goes to Nassima, the amazing photographer on this book. Nass and I met on another project a couple of years ago and it was pretty much love at first sight – a fellow Aussie with zero ego, yet so much talent. I'm honoured to call you my friend and I'm so grateful you were able to be apart of this. I had a very clear vision for this book and you exceeded all of my expectations!

Another massive thank you goes to Lydia the prop stylist. You are just amazing at what you do and I love you to pieces! Thank you for always bringing amazing pieces to the shoot and being so fun to work with. For those of you that aren't in this industry I must explain that working on a book always involves a collaboration of talents. I was very lucky to get such an amazing team together to create a very special type of magic on this book!

And lastly to my assistant Holly, I literally couldn't have done this without you! Thank you for turning up at my flat day after day and dedicating your time to creating delicious cocktails with me. I loved having you there to talk through my ideas and flavour combinations. You are an absolute star and I hope we get more and more jobs where we get to drink delectable cocktails together for weeks on end. Maybe we could do it on location near a beach next time?

Thanks to Emma too, who also assisted on the shoot and thank you all for being very willing 'taste testers' throughout!

Big love,

Nicole xxx